the extra versus ordinary

observations and ideas
for those who want an
extraordinary business

kevin mcmillan

THE EXTRA VERSUS ORDINARY

was written and designed by Kevin McMillan.

www.KevinMcMillan.com

For the Bookshelf, Liam's, Relish, Moonspin,
and many other small businesses in
Thomasville, GA who are extraordinary.

THANK YOU ILY.
You are my greatest encourager and support.

1

Be extraordinary

Every day, we are surrounded by basic, common, boring, typical, bland, mediocre, fair, average things in this world. Most people drive average cars, live in average homes, consume average products, and work in average jobs. Therefore, one would think that there is nothing wrong with having an average company, product, or service.

However, being average is no longer safe, and having a good business is no longer good enough. With the ever-growing amount and availability of competition, people can be picky about who or what they choose and expect more from it. Being average risks invisibility, and duplicating what already exists begs the question, "Do we really need you at all?" The chances for survival as average are ever diminishing.

Something average lacks the ability to stir people's souls. No one is passionate about something they consider ordinary. Instead, they are moved by things that are innovative and insightful; things that bring joy, excitement, pleasure, and satisfaction; things that don't just meet expectations but surprise the customer.

So, if you are going to invest your time, energy, resources, and talents into something, why not make sure it is remarkable? Don't just survive -- thrive. Don't blend in with the crowd -- shine. Don't try stand on the shoulders of others -- soar. Don't settle for average -- be extraordinary!

We have plenty of people involved in the average which creates failed or disappointing results. I don't want to join them (and I hope you don't either). Instead, let's be a part of a growing minority of people who pursue quality and excellence, who dream about creating exceptional products and services, who aren't afraid to try new methods and go against trends, who are willing to break rules and create revolutions, and who want to be remarkable.

If you want to avoid average, then this book was created for you (if not, then hopefully you still have the receipt to return it). ***THE EXTRA VERSUS ORDINARY*** is a collection of my ideas, observations, and commentaries during a two-year period when I was privileged to work with entrepreneurs, leaders, and small businesses in South Georgia and North Florida.

Whether you are just beginning your journey or looking for some more fuel or direction, this book was created to help you reach greater heights. I challenge you to read it frequently asking how you may apply it to your unique situation. Ultimately, my hope is that you will be encouraged, educated, and empowered to be extraordinary!

2

Creating gaps

Back in the 1980s, I started shopping at The GAP. Their clothing (at the time) was conservative and cheap. Unfortunately, every now and then I would notice a girl at school wearing the same shirt as I. That's the risk you take when one side of the store is for women, the other side for men, and everything in the middle is open for debate. Ironically, they called it "The Gap" even though the clothing lines for each sex were a bit blurred. Today, The GAP is quite different, and I no longer panic because I can't figure out which side is the men's.

To be extraordinary, you want a large GAP between you and your competition.

McDonald's and Chick-fil-A both provide fast food, but an obvious GAP exists between how their food quality, marketing, menus, personnel, management, etc. This GAP makes Chick-fil-A stand out from most burger places.

A friend of mine in the construction business expressed his frustration with losing work to competitors who underbid him. If you are in an industry where you compete with bids, you are accustomed to both winning and losing. However, my friend's complaint centers on the fact that the quality of his craftsmanship is considerably higher than others' work, yet those receiving the bids assume everyone's product is of the same caliber. He needs to educate his potential customers about the GAP between him and his competitors.

Are there any gaps between you and your competition? If not, what can you do to create some? If there are, what can you do to better communicate them to your audience?

3

Heated seats

When we bought our Honda Odyssey, I thought the heated seats option was a stupid feature...especially for someone living in South Georgia. Then one day, I turned them on. Actually, the first time was by accident, and I thought something was seriously wrong with me since my rear was getting increasingly hot for no apparent reason. I was quite relieved that it was just the seat and not me.

Ever since then, I always turn them on in the winter and sometimes even when the temperature is as high as 75°. I love having heated seats and can't imagine owning a car without the feature, but I had to try it before I was convinced of its value.

Often, you have to break people's stereotypes and presuppositions with experience. They need to sample who you are or what you do before they are sold. So, the question is, "How do you get people to try?" Word of mouth? Definitely. Free samples? Absolutely. But what else could you do to put them in your seats?

4

Are you smart enough?

We have the smartest customers in history because they have access to more information than ever before (the internet continues to change the rules of marketing and business). Before we purchase an appliance, we may check out Consumer Reports evaluations. Before one buys a book, he/she may read reviews onAmazon.com. Before a family purchases a new car, they may compare prices at KellyBlueBook. Before you see a doctor, you may research your symptoms on WebMD.

This easy access to information means that when someone walks through your door, they may "think" they are as smart as you are. Consumers used to assume that you were the expert. Now, you have to prove it...and proving it is very important because it gives them a sense of security. If you don't appear to be smarter than they are, you will only disappoint, frustrate, or scare them (no one wants an uninformed physician).

Therefore, you (and those working for you) can never say, "I don't know." If you don't immediately have an answer, you had better know where to find it. In other words, you should say, "Let me look into the details of that," instead of "I don't know."

People want a leader, and leaders must have the answers.

5

Hurdles

During my very short time on the high school track team, I never understood why anyone would attempt to run the hurdles. Maintaining the right speed and rhythm was enough of a challenge for me, so why complicate it more by adding something to jump every few yards?

Likewise, your customers will prefer products and experiences that are hurdle-free.

When getting my hair cut, I have to stare at a sign that says, "Please bring correct change. We are not a bank. We cannot make change all day long." HURDLE. I never carry cash because most places (except my barber) take plastic. So, each time my wife tells me that I need a haircut, I have to find some cash...RUN, RUN, JUMP.

The worst part about hurdles is that they are often put in front of us for the businesses' convenience not the customers'. The front door to a local restaurant displays the warning, "WE DO NOT ACCEPT CHECKS." They are probably thinking that they're doing us a favor by sharing this information before we sit down and eat. However, their real motivation is to make sure they don't get stuck with a bad check. What they are actually communicating is, "If you want to eat here, you must jump this hurdle first."

What if you if tried to remove as many hurdles as possible for your customers or clients...even if it meant having more change on hand or getting a few bounced checks? Great products and services originate from walking in the user's shoes.

6

It's as simple as stereo instructions

Have you noticed the evolution of the instruction sheets and booklets that come with technology, furniture, and appliances? We used to joke about how complicated stereo instructions were to understand and follow. Now, most of them come with illustrated (sometimes color) quick-start guides. Before, people either ignored instructions or were frustrated by them.

Today, they are a great example of how to communicate complicated or lengthy information efficiently and effectively. If you have to give guidance or instructions to your audience, make sure it is as simple as stereo instructions.

7

Presuppositions

We all operate under unique assumptions and stereotypes: big corporations are evil; people with English ascents are smart; Japanese cars last longest. Some are based on true events, facts, and experiences while others may be birthed from prejudices, ignorance, and misunderstandings. Regardless whether they are true or not, these presuppositions affect our actions and decisions. Your customers will also approach you with their own presupposed beliefs.

The last thing you want is for people to make inaccurate assumptions of who you are. For example, someone may think your restaurant isn't any good just because your parking lot is empty, or distrust buying your shoes online because you have a poorly designed website, or disregard your plumbing businesses because you have the smallest ad in the Yellow Pages. Sadly, you may have the most amazing restaurant, securest website, or best plumbing service, but people might believe just the opposite because of how you present yourself mixed with their own presuppositions.

You can't control every thought and belief that people have, but you can work to make sure you present the most accurate and honest impression of who you are.

8

Mission critical

There aren't many decorations on submarines. Why? A navy sub has a very critical mission and limited amount of space. Therefore, anything that distracts from or doesn't support the function of a submarine is left behind. What if you managed your company the same way realizing that everything is either a benefit or hindrance to your mission? What would you change or even eliminate?

9

Some flaws are good

Would you search the internet or drive around town to find a mobile food truck AND THEN wait another ninety minutes just to place your order for some "fast food?" Me neither. But then, I've never ordered Korean BBQ from a KOGI truck.

Making it a challenge to find your business is BAD. Long waits to be served is BAD. However, there are rare times when your flaws can actually be assets. KOGI is a perfect example. Customers make the effort to find them and see the search as an adventure. They wait in line and make it an experience because the food is both unique and exceptional. Their chef's resumé boasts of experience in Four-Star restaurants and finishing in the top of his class at the Culinary Institute of America. Plus, he preparing something you can't order at Cracker Barrel: Korean BBQ.

What makes KOGI really remarkable is the whole package. You have to search and wait for a Four-Star chef to serve you Korean BBQ out of a mobile truck so you can sit on the curb and eat it with some new friends. If they were serving McDonald's burgers, it may not work. If they had a truck on every block, it may not work. If there was no social element, it may not work.

Some things that may seem like a flaw by themselves could be the central piece to a well-oiled machine.

10

Innovations versus imitation

I'm tired of hearing American car companies talk about their new hybrids as if they just invented the technology. After twelve years of electric-gas cars on the roads, they should be issuing apologies instead of these "exciting" press releases. There is a big difference between innovation and imitation.

American auto manufacturers are playing catchup while other companies are creating. Take the Toyota Prius for example (which was the first mass-production hybrid vehicle). The third generation Prius hybrid now has instrument buttons and displays that remind you of an a iPod, auto-control assistants to help keep you in the proper lane, it parallel parks for you, and has a solar panel on the roof that provides enough electricity to maintain airflow in the car while it's turned off (i.e., the car is not a baker's oven inside after being parked all day at work).

Toyota is in the innovation business. So is Google. Consider all the online services they have created (or bought): search engines, email, documents, photos, maps, web browser, shopping carts, blogs, chat, video, calendar, translator, 3D drawings, statistics, and more.

The question is, "Are you trying to innovate or just imitate your competition?" Do your customers go "WOW" when you announce or do something new OR are they thinking, "It's about time."

11

Service

My wife and I primarily eat at only a few places in our small town (none of which are chain restaurants). One evening, my father-in-law was visiting one of them and mentioned to our favorite waitress that my wife was at home sick. As he was leaving, she handed him a to-go box with her favorite entree...at no charge! It's hard to find good service today and almost impossible to find extraordinary service like this.

12

Consistency

This weekend, I drove past a sign on the road that said, "Super Huge Sale." The problem is that the sign and words were "super" small. If you are going to say that something is BIG, you can't do it in a small way. You need to be consistent. Make sure that your message matches your mode. The WAY you present something is just as important as WHAT you present. Also, is there really a difference between "Super Huge" and "Huge?"

13

Waiting rooms

Every time I sit in a doctor's waiting room, I know there has to be a better way to make people wait. I have been in hundreds of waiting rooms, and they are all the same: magazines, coffee tables, and chairs. Sometimes there might be a television on, which has never been appealing to me because the receptionist has turned on "Days Of Our Lives" or "The Price Is Right." The worst is when it's on MUTE; what's the point of even having a television that you can't hear?

The waiting room is a missed opportunity.

They have a captive audience, and all they do is hand out worn periodicals (or worse, some boring medical forms to fill out). Magazines are about occupying people's attention so the wait doesn't seem that long. Instead of distracting them while they wait, try focusing their attention on things you want them to know (e.g., information about what you do or offer). Restaurants, are you listening?

Also, remember that no one wants to wait. Another option would be to change the way they feel. How can you make their time enjoyable?

The reality is that doctors are busy, and to them creating a waiting room is like deciding what you need for the front door (a big piece of wood, a door knob and lock, and some hinges). In other words, there is a set formula for waiting rooms, and no one sees any reason to deviate from that.

Gee, thanks Doc!

Every industry has its own set of formulas for how things are done. If you don't care about developing something remarkable, just follow the rules. However,

I challenge you to re-look at how things are being handled. Perhaps, start with a blank sheet of paper and ask how you would design _____ if none existed today.

14

How to say, "Sorry"

It's always a surprise to me when a restaurant runs out of something on their menu...especially when it's one of the main items they serve. Waiters cringe when they hear a customer ordering such an item, and the manager prays that his guest will be forgiving.

Typically, they just respond with, "I'm sorry. We're temporarily out of that."

Without any explanation, I'm going to assume you were dumb enough to let your restaurant run out of food. The worst part is that now I'm pressured to quickly find a new selection while my party waits and the waiter stands over my shoulder.

HOW you say, "Sorry," is important. You can gain support or lose loyalty. If you have to say you're sorry to a customer, be sure to do it in a way that he or she will like you more and not less afterwards. Here are two positive examples:

(1) A few weeks ago at a local café, the waitress informed us that they temporarily removed my favorite item from the menu because the chef was searching for a better beef supplier. Yes, I was disappointed, but I was also impressed that the chef wanted the best quality of meat. Now, I'm anticipating the re-arrival of something I already thought was great.

(2) Another restaurant was out of a key ingredient for a dish I wanted. The chef offered to make something very similar but was not on the menu. Yes, I was disappointed, but now I was getting something special instead of searching for second best.

Don't leave them with "I'm sorry." Give them something more.

15

Make sure you have the right ingredients

During my last year in college, I did an internship which allowed me to work with a psychologist. At first, I thought anyone could do his job since all he did was sit and listen the whole time. Later, I realized that good counselors (and consultants) don't tell people, but they ask the right questions to help people decide what is best to do.

Therefore, here are eight powerful questions that I have used over the years to evaluate different designs, programs, strategies, methods, messages, and more. Some may not apply to all situations, but I think you will find them helpful for your own decisions and directions.

Is it **NECESSARY** (is this influenced by tradition or what is popular, OR is it vital for the present situation)?

Is it **INNOVATIVE** (are there new and better ways)?

Is it **RELEVANT** (does it connect with our audience according to where they are and what they prefer)?

Is it **CLEAR** (is it easily seen and understood)?

Is it **CONSISTENT** (does it match my mission, actions, services, products, appearance, experience, principles, messages, etc.)?

Is it **COMPREHENSIVE** (is it seen or used throughout all or most forms of our communication and marketing)?

Is it **UNITED** (is it working independently or in unison with other parts of our communication and marketing)?

Is it **POWERFUL** (does it stand out and grab attention)?

16

Standing out in a crowd

My mom loves snowmen. We grew up in St. Louis, Missouri, and I have fond memories of making snowmen in our front yard. My parents now live in South Georgia, which suffers from a snow deficit during the winters. So, a few years ago, my dad started a tradition where he gives my mom a new snowman each day during December (none are actually made of snow). The majority are figurines and decorations for inside the home.

Each Christmas, Mom likes to display as many as possible from the past years. As you can imagine, the number of snowmen she has received is now in the hundreds. So, when you walk into their house during December it feels like one of those seasonal gift stores in the mall (but without the price-tags). The problem with so many snowmen displayed all at once is that you really don't notice any one snowman individually. All you see is a huge snow bank of scattered top hats, black coal, and carrot noses.

What if you dropped in one statue of Rudolf with a blinking red noise? You would spot him immediately. He stands out. He shines (literally).

Most people, businesses, projects, and advertising don't SHINE. Why? Because they are floating in a crowded sea of competing companies, ideas, and messages.

Sadly, the default mode for most of us is a general conformity to tradition and popularity. In other words, we tend to do things according to what is accepted and influenced by that which we were exposed to in the past. This default happens on both the personal and professional levels.

For example, you want to start a bank, so based on your experience and knowledge of banks, you determine the hours of operation, interest rates, drive-thru tellers, checkbook options, office arrangements, staff selection, etc. Overall, your bank matches the present standards and actions of banks today. You want a successful bank and this format is how successful banks look and operate. It's what people are familiar with and looking for in a bank.

One problem: we really don't need you. What's the purpose of duplicating what we already have? If you are going to create something, why not meet an unmet need, drastically improve quality and service, offer a unique variation, and/or go beyond common expectations?

I'm sure those starting new businesses believe that their little tweaks or personal touches to the existing model will put them among or just beyond the industry leaders. However, "little tweaks" are a far cry from introducing revolutionary innovations.

I challenge you to start with a blank sheet of paper and ask yourself how you can distinguish your business from others in a major way. Go against tradition. Break the rules. Consider the alternatives that no one considers. How can you be unique in a field of imitators?

Google's homepage is practically naked compared to other search engines who fill your computer screen with links and information. Netflix began mailing DVDs when people were driving to rental stores. Fiji bottled water in a square, boxy container while everyone thought drinks only came in cylinder bottles. So, how can you be unique? How can you shine?

17

Who do we listen to?

You want people to know that your product or service is great. So, what do you do? You tell them. Actually, the first step is to make sure that your product or service really is great. Once it is, then you tell them. There are several different options available, but here are some of the big ones:

(1) The popular method; YOU TELL THEM.

You use create advertising such as television commercials, magazine ads, bumper stickers, and other promo pieces that say, "Hey, we are the best!" This direction is often necessary if no one has even been through your front door, but it tends to be a weak approach. Let me explain. Everyone else is doing the same thing since most people believe this type of advertising is the only option available to them (or they think it's the most effective -- wrong). Sadly, your target audience has hundreds or thousands of other companies yelling at them through advertising.

(2) The expensive method; HIRE A CELEBRITY.

I'm not sure why we think someone in Hollywood knows anything about car insurance or office products (at least they sound better than car dealers who do their own television commercials). I could recommend several other ideas that would generate greater results for less money.

(3) The logical method; USE AN EXPERT.

Any endorsement from someone with "Doctor" in front of their name sounds like a wise choice. If the spokesman is more educated or experienced than we are, he or she must know best (or that is what we tend to tell ourselves). Of course, Americans also think those with English accents sound smarter.

(4) The personal method; LET THEIR FRIENDS AND FAMILY TELL THEM.

We listen to those we trust, connect with, and know the most. Word of mouth is one of the most powerful forms of advertising (but remember that it can be either positive or negative). If you already have a customer/client base (even if it is small), make sure you are empowering them to tell others about YOU.

(5) Lastly, the BEST approach; THEY TELL THEMSELVES.

When a customer tells himself or herself that you are great, it's better than advertising, celebrities endorsements, experts, and friends all put together. You man need to use some of the other approaches above to get to this point, but once there, you need to make sure that they continue to believe it.

There are many other ways to tell people how great you are, but remember that it all starts with BEING great.

18

Like versus love

Why don't you see people with stickers on their cars for Microsoft like you do Apple, and why doesn't anyone sleep outside a new McDonald's the day before a grand opening like with Chick-fil-A?

The answers lie with understanding the difference between "like" and "love." Apple and Chick-fil-A have fans (or fanatics) while Microsoft and McDonald's have customers. It doesn't mean that Apple and Chick-fil-A are better than everyone else, or that no one loves Microsoft and McDonald's.

However, Apple and Chick-fil-A have focused on creating products and services that are beyond the average. Things that people will love. Things that people will go crazy about. Things that people will want to be a part of. It's more than simply producing a product or offering a service. You could say that they are creating a culture that people want to join. You have a choice to create an audience that will either like or love you. Which do you prefer? The choice is yours.

19

Telemarketing versus SPAM

I would like to know who responds to telemarketing phone calls. I never have, but people must buy their stuff to make it profitable. If everyone agreed to NEVER give money to these callers, then their companies would go out of business (no one except our government can survive with a negative income).

Is SPAM any different? NO. Your inbox wouldn't be filled with junk if there wasn't a large enough percentage of recipients that clicked on these emails. Both telemarketing and SPAM interrupts you, offers information you didn't request, and pressures you (perhaps through repetition) to respond or make a purchase.

Isn't there a better way? Of course there is. Perhaps the easiest way to discover it is to do just the opposite.

20

Savoring

One of my physicians told me that I should "savor" meals by eating slowly and focusing on the different flavors, textures, temperatures, etc. I didn't think much of the advice since my wife is an amazing cook, and I have never had any trouble appreciating and enjoying her meals. However, I decided to give it a try. At lunch, Lesli, my wife, had prepared a salad and some bread for lunch. I grew up as a meat-and-potatoes guy and didn't realize that were people who considered salad an entire meal until I met Lesli.

I tried to focus on each bite and to recognize the different flavors. First, the soft spinach bathed with homemade dressing was followed by a crunch of a carrot. Then, there was a surprise when the strong presence of a pecan took charge of the flavor. WOW! I had been eating all my life to fill my stomach more than enjoy the experience -- like putting gas in your car just to make it run. Sure, I always wanted to eat things that I liked (especially pizza), but this was eating on a whole new level.

So, what does this have to do with business? I think we run through tasks and work so quickly that we seldom enjoy events or make them valuable to others.

For example, a healthcare professional was told they could only spend five minutes per patient. That is five minutes to discuss their condition AND the lifestyle changes they would need to make to improve his/her condition. Five minutes to talk about changing one's life! Are you serious? I can't even change the oil in my car in five minutes.

However, this healthcare provider simply has too many patients and not enough staff. My friend eventually left the business because she never could spend her time "savoring" the work she loved, and her patients could never "savor" or appreciate the information provided. It was like asking they to drink from a fire hose. "Sorry. I have no time for any questions. Just take the information and go."

Now compare that situation to the doctor I mentioned earlier who told me to savor my food. The first consultation I had with her lasted two hours (very untraditional for the healthcare field). She intentionally sets aside that much time for every first visit to fully understand the patient's condition. She asked me about my past and present diet, experiences, habits, problems, and treatments as well as future goals and hopes. She believes that you can't treat a small problem or part of a person without understanding the whole of the person. I agree.

When we take a slow and steady approach to things (when we savor them), we can raise their level of quality, enjoyment, service, excellence, value, and more. Savoring is about enjoying, focusing, appreciating, exploring, and evaluating.

Unfortunately, "savoring" is not the norm in business today. Companies don't savor when their phone line is completely automated. Waiters don't savor when they give you the bill a few minutes after the meal is delivered. Sales clerks don't savor when they point you to an isle instead of taking you to the item. Customer Service Departments don't savor when their technicians barely speak your language.

Are you savoring? How can you savor what you do? How can you maintain an environment where people feel comfortable or create an experience in which people feel appreciated? How can you slow down and focus on the moment (or person) in front of you? Maybe you need to start with one of my wife's salads.

21

Will you survive or thrive

I was surprised and disappointed that our government sent "bailout" money to U.S. automakers. There is much debate concerning whether this was the best decision or not. My personal frustration lies with the rhetoric (and underlining belief) concerning helping them survive more than thrive. I continually heard words used such as salvage, persevere, recover, come through, endure, exist, pull through, withstand, and remain viable.

President Obama said in an interview with Bob Schieffer on CBS' "Face the Nation" (3/29/09) that "We THINK we can have a successful U.S. auto industry.

But it's got to be one that's realistically designed to WEATHER this storm and to emerge — at the other end — much more lean, mean and COMPETITIVE than it CURRENTLY IS." Who in America wants to see their tax dollars aid a failing company simply exist and be competitive?

Instead, I want to hear (and support): "We are CONFIDENT that we can have THE MOST successful auto industry IN THE WORLD. But it's got to be one that's RADICALLY designed to SURPASS this storm and to emerge — at the other end — much more lean, mean and EFFECTIVE than IT'S COMPETITORS.

Unless the U.S. auto industry decides that they can (and want to be) the best rather than just a competitor, we might as well start saving now for their next bailout.

22

Emotions are contagious

I find it very insulting when an employee complains about his/her job to me or to one of their coworkers in front of me. They might as well be saying, "My day would be great if you stupid customers would leave." As if I was asking them to do something they were not being paid to do.

Emotions are contagious. Your attitude (and those that work for you) will be associated with your company. If you convey negativity, your customers will have a negative experience. So, either fake a smile if you hate your job, or start checking the want ads.

23

You can only say so much

While eating a bowl of cereal one morning, I began reading the box. There was tons of information crammed on all sides (including the bottom). Some was informative, some funny, some necessary, and some pointless. Most of the time, your audience will not take the time to read everything or even most of it (except those eating a lonely bowl of cereal).

So, how do you determine how much to share?

I believe most people try to "fill the space." Instead, they should ask what is the most important thing(s) they want (or need) to convey. In other words, how much can we take away, NOT how much can we add.

24

Band-Aid marketing

Can we make that BIGGER? What can we fill that u n
u s e d   s p a c e with? How about BOLDING all the
fonts. It needs some ***StArBuRsTs***.

These are just a few of the requests that designers
often hear (and hate). Will making it bigger or bolder
help? Sometimes yes, and there is a proper time and
place for this technique, but often such responses are
"Band-Aids." In other words,   people use them to
cover a problem instead of healing it.

If you are continually having headaches, an aspirin
may relieve the problem for a moment, but why not
ask the question, "Why am I getting headaches in
the first place?"   Alleviate the pain's source. Maybe
you are drinking too much caffeine, or not enough
water, or need better air circulation, or whatever. You
could keep taking an aspirin everyday, or tackle the
source and live aspirin free (NOTE: this is just an
illustration. I don't know anything about headaches
and sympathize with those who suffer from them).

We need to first ask what is wrong (i.e., what are you trying to fix with bigger or bolder), then we can decide what is the best course to correct the problem. Again, first look for the source of your design or marketing problems, then ask how to correct it.

25

You can't handle the truth

Every now and then, my wife asks me to pick up a few things from the grocery store. Most of the time, I will need to call her on the cell phone to verify product specifics. Recently, I was entrusted with the task of buying some hand-soap. Without any detailed instructions or a cell phone, I was on my own to scan the vast selection.

I decided to go with the cheapest and was just about to grab the generic brand, when I noticed a more appealing scent and brand for the same price. Super! But something didn't seem right. Why would this name brand soap have the same price as the generic? The TRUTH was that their prices were identical but their quantities were different. In other words, they were not the same price per volume.

Yesterday, I received a marketing piece in the mail from a local car dealership. It had a lottery style scratch sheet and a car key attached. Restraining my skeptical side, I went ahead and scratched away the surfaces over the three prize boxes and discovered that I WON A NEW CAR!!! I called the phone number listed to confirm it only to hear a recorded voice tell me to go to the dealership, which I did NOT do because I realized that the only thing I had "won" was a chance to visit the dealership and talk to a salesman. Are marketing techniques like these lying?

Technically no. However, to willingly deceive your audience to make a sale is just as bad. Why hide the truth, especially when you know that it will anger people when they learn that you were trying to keep it from them? If your product is really worth more, then price it accordingly. Don't make it seem like it is the same price as everything else.

Plus, don't fool people into visiting your business. Give them real reasons to enter through your front door. Don't set them up for frustration. Even with a legitimate contest, most people are going to be disappointed since more will lose than win. Great products and services should never fear the truth.

26

You got to see, hear, taste, smell and touch this

Like most dryers, ours has an audible alert that sounds a few minutes before a cycle concludes. Unfortunately, the buzzer is loud and irritating, I never want to use it (i.e., I never want to HEAR it). Is it necessary? YES. The purpose of the buzzer is to get my attention so clothes don't sit and wrinkle after the dryer stops. But NO, it doesn't have to be strong enough to wake a bear from hibernation.

If you want to develop a great product or service, be sensitive to the senses.

People experience things by way of sight, sound, smell, taste, and touch. A single dissatisfaction with one sense can lead to overall dissatisfaction. Why didn't the designers of my dryer care that the alert sounded like an air-raid siren? It may be the best dryer to dry clothes, but all I think about is how annoying it is.

Paying attention to the five senses can produce great rewards (and avoid great dissatisfaction). Simply ask, "How will others see, hear, smell, taste, and/or touch this?" Or better yet, "What is the best way for people to see, hear, smell, taste, and/or touch this?"

Sometimes, stimulating a sense not normally associated with your type of product/service can also make you stand out even more (if done correctly). For example, have you ever considered what your office SMELLS like, or why does a mechanic's garage (or himself) have to LOOK dirty and greasy?

Often the sensory experience will play a large part in determining whether you are among the ordinary (average, effective, gets the job done) or EXTRA-ordinary (beyond average, both effective, appealing). So, how do you smell?

27

Color blind

There is a business that sells wood and wood accessories that recently caught my attention, but not in a good way. Their building is primarily made out of wood, which is very appropriate for a "wood store," but the lettering across the top of their roof displaying their name lights up in bright royal blue. It just doesn't look right.

Why not a sign made from wood or if you have to have backlit letters, why not something closer to brown like yellow or tan?

Once, I worked with a team to develop a hospital website. The client wanted to use deep red as the primary color. As a psychologist, I tried to explain theories dealing with color such as recognition and emotions (look up "color psychology" online, and you will learn tons about how different colors can symbolize specific things and invoke unique emotions).

I tried to explain how the color red when used in healthcare tends to makes people think of emergency, alert, danger, or blood, which is NOT the impression you want website visitors to have. Also, red has been known to raise people's heart rate more than any other color.

Color can have powerful effects on people.

Consider the trend setting LIVE STRONG campaign developed by NIKE and their ad agency, Wieden+Kennedy, as an effort to raise funds for the LANCE ARMSTRONG FOUNDATION. As far as I know, they were the first to create plastic wrist bands to show support for a particular cause. I may be wrong about whether they were first, but they definitely produced a worldwide recognized movement.

Professional cyclist Lance Armstrong began wearing the bright yellow band in 2004 to increase cancer awareness, research, and support. Among cyclists, yellow is a significant color. During the Tour de France, the rider with the current best time gets to start the next stage wearing a solid yellow jersey. After battling and surviving cancer, Armstrong came back to win the Tour de France a record-breaking seven times in a row. As you can see, yellow was the perfect color to support his cause and to promote a life where you "Live Strong."

In addition, the yellow really stood out. As a cyclist myself, I started wearing one soon after they went public. People would ask me all the time why I was wearing it and what it meant. It was a great attention getter and conversation starter (before everyone started making their own support wrist bands).

There are good and bad colors to use for your unique business, product, service, and message. Make sure you are using the right colors because the wrong ones can easily distract or detour your audience.

What colors are you painting with?

28

Word of mouth always beats rock, paper and scissors

A few months ago, I was watching a college basketball game with some of my family. Each time the commentators would display a new set of statistics on the television screen or gave the game scores, there was a new company logo to go with it. For example, it's no longer called "Halftime Stats" but now the "Doritos Game Report." Every few minutes before and after commercials, there were more sponsor logos. The station must have sold over fifty spots just for that single game...and I can't recall any of them.

Everyone is trying to get their name/logo out there in as many places as possible. Some will even opt for the smallest overshadowed sticker on a stock car racing in NASCAR. What's the purpose? How much value is there in advertising this way? I think most people subscribe to this "stick-your-name on-anything-that-moves" approach because it's what most businesses do. But what else is there? Ask Audi.

Not long ago, they lent Guy Kawasaki (one of my super heros) a $127,000 Audi sports car for a week. Then, they exchanged it for an Audi Q7 TDI for him to blog about. Why? Because thousands of people read his blog everyday, and Audi knows that the people who read about his experience will tell others, which I am doing right now.

Compare thousands of people talking about your product/service to having a thousand people only catching a glimpse of your logo over some college basketball stat. There's a smarter (and cheaper) way to get your name around town than with stickers.

29

Power of aesthetics

I am on the mailing list for two similar nonprofit organizations who initiated contribution-focused campaigns during the same week. The marketing pieces they sent had identical purposes with roughly the same amount of text. One was a letter, and the other was a brochure. I quickly skimmed over the letter trying get the main point without having to read the whole thing. With the brochure, however, I went through each page consuming ALL of the content.

Why?

The answer is simple. AESTHETICS. The brochure was a non-typical size and printed in full-color with professional imagery throughout. They used different font colors and sizes to draw the reader into the text and communicate their message. On the other hand, the letter was printed on their typical stationary with no extra imagery, color, or expression. It looked and felt like a hundred other legal documents and emotionless statements I get from banks, insurance agencies, and credit card companies.

Layout, color, imagery, and other elements of aesthetics can play a critical role between success and failure in communication. The quality of design often determines how many people will listen to your message and how they will feel about it. If you don't give design special attention, your marketing may end up in the trash next to credit card offers.

30

Who am I?

Designing a company website can be an extremely difficult project mainly because you have to create an online experience, copy, and design that matches the company's identity. This task is nearly impossible when a company doesn't have a clear view of who they are or have written and visual elements to represent them. The first step I take in web design or consulting is to research both the client and their specific industry.

Then, I prepare proofs according to how I see and understand them. Sometimes, the client shakes his head in disappointment because it just doesn't look right to him. This result often means that either they are not able to effectively articulate who they are OR they themselves don't know who they are. Sometimes, working with committees and teams amplifies the problem since each person could have a different view of their mission or brand.

You will continually run into issues like this if you don't take the time to decide who you are and make sure you have communicated this message clearly to everyone.

31

Will the croc become extinct?

With the ever-increasing popularity of reading content (e.g., news, books, blogs, tweets) on devices such as the Blackberry, iPhone, iPad, and Kindle, are we witnessing the slow death of books? My wife and I were talking about this trend with a friend of ours who owns a remarkable small-town bookstore. It was inevitable that the movie "You've Got Mail" would come up during our conversation.

As you may know, Meg Ryan plays Kathleen Kelly, the owner of a children's bookshop who is having to deal with the fierce competition of a mega bookstore that opened nearby. Sadly, she eventually resigns to having lost and closes the store. Why did she fail (beside the fact that the movie writer wanted it this way) even though she put up a good fight and rallied television exposure and activists to her cause?

I know this is a fictional story, but her response is very typical today. Her flaw has to do with the common belief that advertising alone can save you. Unfortunately, how are you going to "out advertise" someone bigger and better funded than you? Rather than pouring a lot of time, energy and money into an advertising campaign, consider changing your service, product, or experience to be better than your competition.

Let me give you an example. Over the past year or two, CROCS shoes has had a surge in popularity. Whenever I see a product (especially a line of clothing) climb to great heights over a short period of time, I wonder how long it will take before it falls into the "popularity black-hole" that swallowed up Jams, Parachute Pants, Member's Only jackets, and other things that I owned during the 1980s.

Can CROCS avoid extinction?

YES, but they must EVOLVE, which appears to be their current strategy. They now make more than the simple plastic clog. You can get different variations of clogs, sandals, flip-flops, casual shoes, and more. Another approach open to them is to focus on creating an allegiance with a very specific audience who will never leave them even when their popularity fades.

Take Birkenstocks for example. They had a huge following in the 90's, which eventually faded. However, they also built a loyal following (that includes me) who still wear their shoes because they created something that was more than a fad. In other words, their product had a foundation that was able to withstand the ever-changing wind of style.

To survive, you can't just sit there and hope you will be eternal. It's survival of the fittest where those that evolve last longest (maybe Darwin should have gone into marketing).

32

Give them a reason

I'm not a fan of most chain restaurants (I'll save my reasons why for another day). My culinary love is dedicated to the small private eateries. However, I will probably never visit the two independent restaurants that have recently opened in my area.

Why? They have failed to give me a good reason to try them.

The first has opened in the building that was once occupied by a fast-food burger and fries chain that failed locally. Sadly, they are serving basically the same menu. I would have loved to ask them before they opened why they thought they would succeed where someone who had more experience, reputation, and support failed. Since they look very similar to most fast-food places, you assume their menu is no different from the competition. Why would I ever go there? Curiosity? Maybe. You want something new? Perhaps.

Unfortunately, neither one of these reasons are strong enough, and both are very risky since people will not return unless your food and/or service is better than everyone else's. In other words, you must have a dynamic first impression that motivates the customer to return and tell others. You will never have a first impression if you can't give people a compelling reason to try your business.

The second restaurant is even worse. Not only are they also trying to make it in a place where two previously restaurants have closed, but they are located at least fifteen miles from town (any town). Since they have failed to tell me anything about themselves other than they are a grill-type restaurant, I would have to be very, very curious and willing to take a risk to drive that far not knowing what the experience will be like.

What should they do?

Give people a reason to visit them other than curiosity. They need to show that they have the best (or unique) service, food, experience, prices, or any thing that sets them apart from the rest. If people can get the same thing from somewhere else that they have been before, they probably will.

33

Renovation without innovation

A local restaurant closed a few months ago for renovations. When they reopened, they unveiled a new sign and interior furnishings. However, the "improvements" were identical to their past sign and furniture. In other words, they didn't make the establishment better only cleaner. Like giving an old dog a bath, they just replaced old stuff with new, but it still feels like an old dog.

If you are going to renovate something, do so with some innovation. Make it better, more exciting, more effective. In other words, IMPROVE IT. Don't just clean it - enhance it. Otherwise, you simply inconvenience your customers for your spring cleaning.

34

What can I get you to drink?

Over the past years, I have been watching the progress, competition, and differences between brands of bottled water (I'm a big water drinker, and YES, Fiji water is the best...or so the marketing tells me). Recently, I had an interesting conversation with the innovator behind RedFin energy drinks. As a dedicated H2O consumer, I was unaware of the vast selection of "power packed" drinks. Hundreds of brands and variations are available today.

Here are just a few that I found online in a couple of minutes: 5-hour Energy, Punch, Rockstar Energy, Jolt Cola, Monster Energy, Red Bull, Skinny Gazelle, Full Throttle, Hype, KMX, and Guru. The developers range from multibillion dollar beverage companies to college students (even Steven Seagal has one on the shelves called Lightning Bolt).

Now consider the "Cola Wars" that have been going on for years. This struggle is primarily between just two companies, Pepsi and Coca-Cola. They have probably spent as much money battling each other as the U.S. and the Soviet Union did during the Cold War. They have gone through multiple celebrities, lawsuits, labels, commercials, events, and more. Coca-Cola even altered their formula only to bring it back a few months later. Pepsi spent over a billion dollars (that's a lot of zeros) rebranding their entire product line recently. I wonder what would have happened if instead they choose to reduced the price on a billion or so Pepsi cans down to 5 cents. I bet you would get more new Pepsi drinkers that way for the same price.

So, who will be the winner? Will it be the one with the best product, packaging, ingredients, taste, attention to their audience, selection or flavors, ability to stand out from the others, or martial artist endorsing their product?

Here's my advice: don't worry about winning or battling the competition as much. Instead, make your top priority to produce the best product you can! Maybe you can even get me to start drinking something besides water.

35

Election marketing

I have been excessively frustrated with the past few elections as the influence of marketing is evident more than ever. Are we voting for the candidate or the PR, design, and media people behind them? It's hard to separate the two today since marketing and communication are the vehicles that tell us about the people. This trend doesn't exist just in Washington. I heard a report the other day that Hollywood now spends more on marketing movies than they do making them.

So, what's the problem?

Eventually, we are so blinded by the power marketing that we are no longer concerned with the quality of product or person we are promoting. As consumers, we become so dependent on marketing and media to tell us what to believe that we stop thinking.

The sad conclusion is that quality continues to go down and down. Hollywood is less concerned with making a great movie and more concerned with whether they can sell it (this is why you see so many sequels and remakes). Washington becomes filled with those who hired the right people to make them look good despite who they really are. In a few years, I could probably get my dog elected.

36

Everyone needs a little marketing

For some people, marketing sounds like a bad word... especially if you are wanting to apply it to certain things such as religion or faith. But, is marketing bad? Well, as one of my grad school professors liked to say, "YES and NO."

The only way to accurately answer this question is to ask "What type of marketing is it?"

I see two large categories of marketing. The first is focused on getting people to respond the way

YOU want them to (buy my product). The second is concerned with helping people respond the way THEY want to (here is the service you are looking for). The best marketing, in my opinion, is the latter option where people (not YOU) come first.

Life is made up of relationships (even Tom Hanks formed a relationship with a volleyball when left alone on an island). The key to any successful relationship is good communication (not money) and putting the other(s) before yourself. Marketing is strategic communication. Therefore, good marketing should focus on improving communication, serving your customers/clients, and understanding your audience.

People want marketing. Of course, they would never use the word, but people want better ways to communicate, listen, and understand. What they don't want are gimmicks, tricks, spam, pushing, or deception. Again, the question is what type of marketing are you doing?

37

Know thy audience

If I was to make ten commandments of marketing, then "Know Thy Audience" would be one of them. Businesses and organizations continually violate this simple yet important rule. When my son was nine month old, he had to take a vitamin supplement. At this age Chewable Flintstones won't work, so it had to be a liquid. But does it have to taste, smell, and look terrible? If we can make organic donuts, I'm sure it's possible to create liquid vitamins that are pleasant tasting for infants.

So, why didn't this company make a better vitamin? Was it cheaper not to? Perhaps. But I think the real barrier was that they didn't know their audience. If they could have witnessed my son spraying his mom and me with the first taste of their medicine, maybe they would have made taste a priority in their development. The point is that we sometimes get so involved with the money, production, and other things that we forget about who is using our product or service.

38

Everything Is an opportunity

A local company was overcharged for a meal at a neighboring restaurant. Later, the bookkeeper informed the manager of the billing error by his staff. His response was to just refund the charge.

Every interaction you have with your customers is a chance to increase satisfaction, and most importantly, build loyalty. Failures especially should be used to nurture and solidify the relationships with your audience. It's been said that you know someone best NOT by how they act but by how they RESPOND.

When this manager discovered the extra charge added to their lunch, he could have offered to do more than correct the cost. Doing the minimum required may fix the problem, but it doesn't remove the customer's frustration or compensate for his/her inconvenience.

No matter how you respond, people are going to share their experiences with others. It will either be as complaints or praises. Why have their story end with, "and all he did was refund my money" when it could be, "then they delivered free deserts to our office!"

39

A little better

While pumping gas at a local BP station, I noticed a small advertisement that literally said they were a "little better" than the average gas station. It even had a website link (www.ALittleBetterGasStation. com). The problem was that they really weren't any better than most gas stations around. In fact, they were one of the oldest and cheapest (not in price).

Furthermore, why state that you are only a little better? If you are going to take the time and money to make a statement, why not say your are A LOT BETTER gas station...or even THE BEST gas station? Truth is that BP sent them the sign, they displayed it, and no one cared whether it was true or even worth sharing.

40

Filtered marketing

Several years ago, a client of mine was planning a big event to bring families closer together. During one particular meeting, someone suggested hosting a community picnic. When they mentioned the word "picnic," everyone began sharing thoughts about picnics (e.g., hotdogs, paper plates, music). Unfortunately, none of these "picnic plans" had anything strategic to do with bringing families closer together.

They forgot their ultimate mission and became consumed with planning a great picnic. They should have asked, "How do we use a picnic to draw families closer together?" They could have prevented this course drift entirely by comparing each idea and suggestion to the mission and thus ensuring that every decision was working toward the end goal.

You should make decisions like a filter. A filter separates, suppresses, absorbs, or removes something unwanted from the parts you want to keep. Air filters block dust to ensure the air is clean to breathe. Water filters take away dangerous particles to provide pure drinking water. SPAM filters quarantine emails that may contain hazardous viruses to protect computers. So, in a similar manner, you can "purify" all your decisions, goals, tasks, and actions by "filtering" them through your mission and principles.

Filtering keeps you on track, but it also allows you to make decisions quicker and easier. Each day is filled with numerous tiny decisions and actions. They may not seem very critical, but if each one is not checked, then little compromises can begin to add up over time creating major changes. Just one degree off course can mean the difference between whether your plane lands in Europe or Africa. Filtering ultimately preserves and protects who you want to be in the present and the future.

The next time you have to buy something, hire someone, respond to a customer, create an advertising piece, pick a color of paint, or answer the phone, ask yourself if this action or decision will propel you toward or lead you away from your main objective(s)? Otherwise, you may be drinking dirty water.

41

"WOW" has an expiration date

My mother-in-law served some new chocolate treats last Christmas. They were so delicious that I was tempted to eat the whole tray. Two weeks later, I had some more at her house (another delightful experience). Then, she gave me a whole pack to take home. Since then, however, I have enjoyed them with a mixed pleasure. I know that in a few days the treats won't be so amazing. The more I eat them the less special they become.

"WOW" can expire when it becomes common, easy, available, and/or abundant.

Consider the appeal of Starbucks. Even with the extraordinary rate of early growth, Starbucks used to be a rare and exciting find. Today, they seem to be everywhere. Their coffee beans are sold in grocery stores. Many restaurants serve it to their customers. Retail stores, such as Target, have small stands at their entrances. Of course, you can find thousands of their main shops throughout the world. The coffee may still be good, but it is no longer a unique surprise to find or enjoy.

Here's another example:

Often at restaurants the manager will come by our table towards the end of our meal to see how we are doing. Extraordinary? No...or not anymore at least. At one time, it may have been seen as something special. Now, it is simply the way most restaurants operate...like handing out menus. There's nothing remarkable about it. If a manager did something out of the ordinary, such as giving one lucky table a free desert each night, then the action would be special.

Continually evaluate who you are and what you do to make sure your WOW hasn't expired.

42

Consider doing the opposite

One of my favorite episodes of the television series "Seinfeld" centers on George Costanza's decision to do the complete opposite of his natural instincts. By doing so, everything seems to start going right in his life (e.g., new girlfriend, job with the New York Yankees, and moving out of his parents' house).

We often make decisions based on tradition, feelings, popularity, and peer pressure. What if we considered doing the opposite? Consider these examples from the past:

TESLA MOTORS: Electric cars are small, slow, and goofy looking. WHAT IF we made one that was a sports car?

CHICK-FIL-A: Fast-food is prepared quick and cheap, therefore quality and service can be sacrificed. WHAT IF customer service and satisfaction were our top priorities?

GOOGLE: Computer programs for things such as word processing, spreadsheets, and email run from software you install on your computer hard-drive. WHAT IF we made it possible for people to access and use such programs online from any computer?

NETFLIX: Video rental stores focus their inventory primarily on new releases, fluctuate rates based on length of rental and release date, and charge late fees. WHAT IF we eliminated the physical store entirely and send the videos directly to homes, change the pricing philosophy, and try to make the video selection unlimited?

LANDSEND: Retailers will not accept returns for items that have been worn, washed, used, or in any condition other than how it was when bought. WHAT IF we allowed our customers to return things no matter what the reason, condition of the product, or amount of time they owned it?

Sometimes doing the opposite can create the extraordinary.

43

Lessons from my barber

The barber shop I visit every few months (after my wife has repeatedly commented on the "shagginess" of my hair) is really terrible. The shop is old and ugly. The wait is usually long (no appointments). The chairs are incredibly uncomfortable which makes the wait even worse. The magazines are old...and I don't mean last month old...these are a few YEARS old. The conversation with the barber is sometimes awkward, plus he doesn't take credit cards or make change.

So why do I go back and refuse to go anywhere else? It's simple. There are two things I love about my barber that overshadow all his limitations: Price and Results. A haircut there is only $7, and I like the way he cuts my hair more than any previous barber. He takes his time to make sure everything is perfect even if there are many people waiting. He goes the extra mile by trimming my eyebrows and beard.

In addition, he uses a straight razor on the back of my neck for an extra close trim. Other barbers have charged me seven times as much for half the service. Sometimes you can still be great even though you have some major flaws. Why not tackle the flaws also and move from being great to AMAZING?!

44

Your ambassadors

Whether you like it or not, your employees, volunteers, and even customers are your ambassadors. They carry banners that continually make statements about your organization or business.

For example, I drove past one of those "sign guys" this weekend (people standing on street corners holding posters promoting some big sale or event). It was pouring rain, and this guy was wearing a plastic trash bag in a poor attempt to stay dry. My first thought was, "What a jerk his employer is for making him stand out in the rain."

Not all advertising is good.

Later that night, we ate dinner at a unique café where we received below-average service from our waiter. He never refilled our drinks and visited so infrequently that we had to ask two other waitresses for things. Worst of all, while we were in need of napkins or more water, we could see him behind a half-wall sitting and talking with other staff.

I admit that with two small children and having ordered water instead of wine, we didn't look like big tippers or easy customers. Yet, such an assumption should never be the standard for the quality of service you deliver (then again, he could have been a lousy waiter for everyone). Ironically, I ended up tipping him 30% in hopes that it would make some nonverbal statement about service or assumptions.

What is the message your ambassadors are carrying?

P.S. -- People are not the only ambassadors you have. Your website, email, signs, ads, music, food, receipts or invoices, voicemail, uniforms, climate, furniture, and Christmas cards also represent who you are.

45

"Eat Mor Chikin"

I love Chick-Fil-A (actually, I have never eaten at one since I have a poultry allergy). However, their approach to business, marketing, and customer service is so good that I will risk the swelling and hives for the sake of my kids.

From their "cows" to giving employee scholarships, Chick-Fil-A continually impresses me. While waiting for our local fireworks show to start, the operators of our town's Chick-Fil-A went around handing out special glasses (like the 3D paper glasses) that would "enhance" seeing the colorful explosions. They made me a bit dizzy to wear, but every kid around me had them on when the show started, and THEY LOVED IT!

Chick-Fil-A is more than a fast-food restaurant...it's an experience, and perhaps even a culture of good customer service. Plus, what other restaurant has "fans?" Oh, I wish that I could eat "chickin."

46

Do you believe in evolution?

After our second child was born, my wife and I decided it was time to swallow our pride and buy a minivan (more kids require more space). I quickly zeroed in on the Honda Odyssey and started researching the differences between the models they have released since 1998.

Over the past ten years, Honda has made major upgrades to the look and/or features of their minivan at least three times (1999, 2005, and 2008). Why change...especially in 2005 when their 2004 rating from Consumer Reports was the highest they had received?

A client of mine stresses the importance of continually creating, capturing, and sustaining momentum in church ministries. When you have a spike in attendance or involvement after a church event, you need to "capture" that momentum, "sustain" it, and then repeat the process by "creating" new momentum generating events.

Their strategy can ring true in business and marketing. To insure the survival of your service or product, you need to "evolve" (slow and strategic improvements over time). Consider the progression of Apple. They have progressed from the production of a personal computer (once targeted at educational institutions) to selling music and videos online, MP3 players (the iPod), cell phones, and now tablets. Apple fans read magazines, websites, and blogs in search for the latest Apple product or innovation from Steve Jobs.

Do you believe in evolution? Are you improving your services, enhancing the features of your product, or streamlining your organization? If not, you may soon be facing extinction.

However, be careful. Change is also risky. The 2005 Honda Odyssey received the lowest rating from Consumer Reports than any other year so far. Yet, there is a greater risk with staying the same and expecting continued success.

47

Don't talk to strangers

My wife and I used to talk about opening a coffee shop. There are several reasons why we haven't, but it's mostly because I DON'T DRINK COFFEE. Oh, I love the environment (and smell) of a coffee shop, but how will I ever understand and appreciate my product or customers as a water drinker?

Be very cautious about trying to serve, sell or market to a group of people you don't understand or relate well with. One of the easiest ways to avoid the potential pitfalls of not understanding your audience is to target people and groups like yourself. Maybe, I should open a water shop.

48

Signs and more stupid signs

Is it smart to hire someone to stand on a street corner and waive a sign to promote your business, sale or event? It depends. The rule to remember is that the people and signs used will represent YOU.

Recently, a local oil change center had two uniformed employees smiling and waiving at people driving by - GOOD. A furniture store going out of business chose to hire non-employees who held their signs while drinking, talking on cell phones, and intent on never smiling or making eye contact - BAD.

HOW you present your message is just as important as WHAT you present.

I don't care for people waiving and displaying signs on the street's edge. If you're going to do it, make sure they give the impression you want people to have of your service or product. Which is better...a high school student talking on his cell phone while waving a sign for your business OR saving the money and just sticking the same sign in the ground?

I have to admit that someone on a street corner waving a sign briefly grabs your attention, but that's not my complaint. I get frustrated at the missed opportunities and when people don't strive for excellence or the extraordinary. The sign wavers I saw this week promoting a new Halloween store in town missed a huge opportunity. They were waving small signs (instead of using large sandwich boards) and were dressed in jeans and T-shirts (instead of Halloween costumes)!

Again, which is better...teenagers with soft drinks and your business sign OR Dracula and Frankenstein holding a store banner? If you are going to interrupt people with your message, make sure it's done in a powerful, excellent, or fun way.

49

Do they have the right stuff?

A client of mine continually complains about the people working under him. I understand his frustration because your marketing and communication is only as good as the people involved with it.

However, as a leader you never have the right to complain about your team or staff.

They are your responsibility (and so is their work). You can either accept their performance, work to improve it, or find someone else for the job. Complaining only reveals your lack of action, responsibility, or understanding your role.

Having the right people working for you is still very important. They have the power to enhance or destroy who you are and want to be. Therefore, evaluate, train, and encourage your team. Here are a few questions that might help:

(1) Do they understand the basic principles of communication, marketing, advertising, etc.?

(2) Are they qualified for the tasks they have been assigned?

(3) Are they all working under the same goals, principles, and standards?

(4) Do they have a clear understanding of who does what?

(5) Is there one central person who knows all that is happening that people can go to with issues?

(6) Do they know when to use in-house personnel versus outside professionals/vendors?

(7) Are they using their primary talents and abilities?

(8) Do they enjoy what they are doing?

(9) Are they maintaining what was done the previous year or advancing forward?

(10) Am I the right person to lead them?

50

Wrapping Paper

"Never judge a book by its cover." True, but if you're like me, you usually do. Even though I have read good books with bad covers and bad books with good covers, I still assume some books will be good or bad simply based on the cover design.

Wrapping paper matters...it sets our expectations.

A nostalgic "soda-fountain" shop closed for renovations. Those in the town couldn't wait for the reopening and had high expectations. The unveiled changes looked wonderful. Unfortunately, the food didn't reach such heights. What could have been a popular place now seems to be an average restaurant?

Unmet expectations breed discontent, frustration, and disappointment (three words you never want associated with your service, company, or product). If you wrap something in pretty paper, be sure it's worthy of the present inside.

51

Change

My brother-in-law was telling me last weekend about his trip to Central America. One of the highlights was his discovery that Coca-Cola down there tastes like the old, original COKE (before they introduced "NEW COKE" and later "COKE CLASSIC").

Why did Coca-Cola decide to change its taste when that was the primary reason why people chose it? Was it because of Money...Marketing...or perhaps both? Tombstone pizzas used to be the best tasting frozen pizza on the market (in my opinion) until the company was bought out by Kraft who changed the cheese. Why did they change the star ingredient?

I'm a BIG believer in changing things, BUT ONLY if it is for the purpose of improvement, and NOT for the sake of more sales or spending less in production. Seek profits first, and you will be tempted to compromise. Seek to provide a great service or product, and profits will follow.

52

Little things

Several years ago, I was surprised to receive two packages in the mail from a local car dealership shortly after buying one of their SUVs. The first gift was a car wash kit. The second was a set of folding chairs that matched my new car.

Even though the cost of the gift was nominal compared to the price I paid for the gas-guzzling, oversized SUV, it magically made me feel like I was getting a bonus or bargain. Why? The reason was because no other car dealership had ever done anything like this for me in the more than ten times I've bought a new car. It was also a brilliant marketing action because every time I use the car wash kit or chairs (which I still have and use), I think of that dealership.

Every time you communicate with your audience, it is a MARKETING OPPORTUNITY. It's usually the little things that make the BIG differences.

53

Wally World

I can't stand going to Wal-Mart. There are a number of reasons why, but the main reason is that they never impress me. Seldom do I find a helpful employee or a plentiful selection or extraordinary products. It's just a large warehouse full of cheap products, long lines, undereducated staff (or at least that's how they make me feel).

What if Wal-Mart asked, "How can we create a dynamic shopping experience WHILE providing economical products?" Of course, I need to remind myself of one of my own marketing principles: Something for everyone is something for no one. Perhaps Wal-Mart just isn't for me OR maybe they just aren't trying.

54

Terms & conditions

I never read the "Terms & Conditions" companies have me agree to before downloading their product (e.g., a song or software). Maybe you do. I have a feeling that most companies either don't care if you do and only have it there to protect themselves, OR they don't realize that this is a poor way to communicate an important message. If you want people to read, understand, and care about what you have to say, then present it in a manner that is more appealing and compelling.

55

Classic versus junk

The state of Georgia has a specialty license plate available for classic car owners. Besides having to pay an extra fee, I don't believe there are any restrictions or criteria placed on who can purchase one. Every now and then, I will see some old, beat-up vehicle with one of these classic plates, but I never would never consider the car to be a "classic." Just because something is old, doesn't mean that it is also classic.

Make sure your perception lines up with others. Just because YOU think something is great doesn't mean others will also. It's easy to get lost in our own high view of ourselves and remain ignorant to how others see us. The most dangerous time is at the beginning of a new business when you think EVERYONE will find your product or service to be as great as you do. In reality, no one will love you as much as you or your mom. Start small and slowly. Listen to the opinion and comments of others. And, make sure you really are a classic if you are wearing that name tag.

56

Let's make a great toaster

I hate my toaster, which I bought because it was the cheapest. However, I pay the "price" for that decision each morning when I make bagels for breakfast. The toaster never lifts the bagels (or any type of sliced bread) high enough out of the toaster, which forces me to reach into the super HOT toaster to retrieve my breakfast. It's like playing the game OPERATION where a slight shake of the hand results in a loud buzzer (or in this case burnt fingers).

The toaster company probably sacrificed design for the cheaper price tag, and I sacrificed quality to save a few extra bucks. Is it possible to make an affordable AND great toaster? I don't know since I'm not in the toaster business. However, I do believe we would have better products and services today if people were asking the right questions.

How about YOU? Could you have a better product or service? Are you making sacrifices?

57

I thought I saw a tweedy bird

I've noticed that every time I see a bluebird illustration, I think of Twitter. Hundreds of variations have been created of Twitter's "tweedy bird," which people immediately recognize and associate with Twitter. You would have to say that they have developed a great brand, but what is a brand?

Some like to think of it as a name, trademark, or logo. Others will unfold long theories about psychological perceptions and visual experiences. I tend to fall somewhere in the middle by using the word interchangeably with "identity." In other words, a brand is your business identity.

This identity is often represented by your name, phrases, jingles, people, mission statement, experiences, and more. To think of a brand as a just your logo would be like saying that my car or clothes reflect exactly who I am. Yes, they are surely part of it, but there is much more to me than what I own. It's easy for companies to go to either extreme of thinking too much or too little about their brand.

The most important thing to remember is that the symbols which represent your company can both remind people of who you are (what they already know, believe, or feel about you) as well as make new statements (what people will assume about you from these symbols). This recognition is important because you need to continually make sure that the messages are consistent with who you are and what you want to be.

The first step is to decide on who you are, and then you move on to the things you choose to represent and explain you. So, who are you?

58

Increased rates

A few companies that I use have increased their rates over the past year, and they all did it the wrong way. My insurance agent sent a long letter about how rates will always increase; my primary media supplier gave no warning or explanation probably hoping no one would notice; and a music company tried to make me feel sorry for their financial situation and said they had no choice but to pass the cost on to ME.

Price increases are a fact of life. The changes in the economy and our lives affect the cost of business. I don't have a problem with that fact. Just be mindful of how you present these changes to your audience. If you allow the message to focus entirely on the negative ("We don't have any choice but to charge you more for the same exact service"), then your customers may stop to consider whether the product or service is worth the new cost.

Instead, you want to reinforce their decision to choose you over everyone else. Can you offer them some type of bonus or addition to justify the new rate/price? How can you make your product/service seem even more valuable than before? If you have to bear such bad tidings be sure to do it in the most positive way possible.

59

The nice guy

When shopping alone, I often have customers mistake me for a store employee (wearing a red shirt and khakis at Target doesn't help). Why me? I think my high school yearbooks can give some insight. Mine was filled with comments such as "You're such a nice guy" or "Stay sweet." In addition, I was voted by my senior class as "The Best Dressed of 1991." You put the these two things together and you have the perfect employee people look to for assistance.

We all would prefer getting help and service from someone with a happy or optimistic demeanor. The manager of a Ritz Carlton in Florida once told me that he could train people to do just about anything but be nice. If someone wasn't a genuinely nice person from the start, he/she was automatically disqualified as a prospective employee.

In addition, appearance makes a statement about performance. Though often unfounded, people automatically think that someone clean and well dressed will be more knowledgeable, pleasant, or helpful than someone with a shabby appearance. How is your team? Are any of them candidates to be the nicest or best dressed employee of the year?

60

Don't design like NASCAR

Whenever I design a communication or marketing piece (e g , website, ad, brochure), I always ask, "How much can I strip away from this and still communicate the main point(s)?" My intention is to streamline each design to allow the main point to surface above everything. Sadly, many of my clients have preferred to add as much information as possible believing that people will read everything they write (their advertising pieces look like NASCAR vehicles all covered with stickers).

We have been bombarded with so much advertising over the years that we have conditioned ourselves to ignore it. So why do you want to add to the clutter by overloading your own marketing? You need to communicate your message quickly, easily, and effectively. Begin by asking, "What is the most important thing to convey?" Then, take away everything else that isn't necessary and/or distracts from the main point.

Another thing to note here is that only the biggest sponsor logo on a NASCAR is noticed, if any at all. Therefore, don't waste your money on small advertising that will easily be swallowed up by larger things around it.

61

Did it really save money?

My cell phone has been giving me some problems, so I called the company tech support line. After a long wait, I was connected with a customer service rep who was clearly not from or in the United States. In the end, I had to endure three separate one-hour phone conversations with people who barely spoke English, wait several days for parts to be mailed to me (twice), and eventually receive a replacement phone that still doesn't work.

Why? Because we were all trying to save money.

I bought this prepaid phone because I didn't want a costly phone contract, and the company I bought it from outsourced their tech support overseas because it was cheaper to have people in another country read scripts and follow predetermined steps.

Did we really save money?

Time is money. I spent too much time trying to work out my phone issues, and now I have to spend more time canceling my service and looking for a new phone company. For the phone company, it may be cheaper to use services outside the U.S., but how many customers are they losing as a result of this decision.

Are you doing anything to save money that in the long run is costing you?

62

Making the common exceptional

I would love to drive a Ferrari, but life is easier owning a minivan when you have three kids. The requirements and restrictions of my family lifestyle (e.g., price and number of seats) match a minivan a hundred times more than a Ferrari. This isn't much of a surprise, but why doesn't someone make a truly exceptional minivan? When compared to every other van on the market, mine isn't extraordinary (except that it is Ferrari red).

When Volkswagon, one of my favorite car companies, announced they would be releasing their take on the family van a few years ago, I was hoping (and expecting) for a van that would shake things up (maybe a hybrid or high performance or something with more road clearance for families who camp but don't want an SUV). Sadly, their minivan looks and operates very similar to my Honda. In other words, they decided to imitate rather than innovate and ended up with another average van.

Most people consider the minivan to be an average vehicle. In other words, they don't expect it to be exceptional since it is made for hauling kids to soccer games, getting groceries, and taking family trips to the beach. The style and features are now much the same: sliding doors, a DVD player, plenty of seats, cup holders, and space for luggage.

Why stop there?

Make a really amazing minivan by going outside the minivan equation; break some rules; ruffle some feathers. Adding extra cup holders or another DVD player doesn't take you from the common to exceptional. You have to rethink the norm or try something completely new. Then, perhaps, my single friends will stop making fun of me for driving a minivan.

63

Communication is everywhere

You may not realize it, but you are actively involved in communication every day (and you can't turn it off). Everything we do communicates something to those who see, hear, and experience it. We tend to think of communication in terms of planned actions, such as developing a sermon podcast, running a magazine ad, or displaying banners at an event. However, communication is wider and deeper than that.

You are continually expressing, even if it is unintentional, things about yourself to those around you. In turn, these people will make judgements about your beliefs, intentions, preferences, or feelings based on "clues" from even your smallest actions (or inactions) and decisions. Your choice of room temperature, style, office hours, "paper or plastic," and logo colors are all communicating messages, maybe not as directly but sometimes just as powerfully, as multimillion-dollar television commercials. It is not a choice of ARE you going to communicate but a question of HOW and WHAT you will communicate.

Since communication is everywhere, so are thousands of opportunities to share a specific message with your audience. You can pay little attention to minor details OR strategically look at everything as a new chance to make a statement. Remember that most things will communicate something about you whether you want them to or not. So, why not make sure they are presenting an accurate and powerful message?

Try this: During the day write down everything you see that could communicate a message to those who encounter your business. Then, list what that message was AND what you want it to be.

64

Decide whose way it will be

Two local businesses are using two completely different communication approaches to reach the same audience. One has opted to use social media services while the other still relies on traditional methods. The first is trying to use means that are most popular with their audience while the latter employs techniques that they are personally most comfortable with. Is one way better than the other?

You can choose to connect with your audience through methods that you like best OR select ways your audience prefers. The former option is not very "customer centric," and you will begin to alienate certain groups who don't want to communicate your way. In addition, by conforming to your audience's preferences, you extend your reach and impact. As a result, you will connect with a higher percentage of your audience.

However, using forms of communication that you are not comfortable with can lead to other problems, mostly associated with quality. There are benefits and drawbacks to both directions. You almost have to choose between connecting with more people or using your most comfortable approach (or one that was previously successful). You must decide one way or the other. Otherwise, you will find yourself doing both and not being as effective in either.

65

Lost in the translation

One day at a post office in Orlando, Florida, I heard two people speaking German, another on her phone in French (I think it was French; I don't speak French, so I don't know), and the clerk behind the counter conversing fluently with customers in both Spanish and English. Orlando is a very international and diverse place.

However, I knew a pastor there who continually talked about American Southern culture, especially football.

I often wondered if he was able to really connect with those he was trying to reach (especially the Europeans who think football is what we know as soccer).

You need to know WHO you are trying to reach, WHAT they are like, WHERE they are from, and HOW they communicate. In other words, you need to relate and be relevant to your audience. Relevance deals with the complete environment in which you operate. You should evaluate more than your audience. Are you relevant in your location, mission, identity, workplace, staff, product, service, customer experience, communication, and advertising?

Also, being relevant requires understanding present techniques, trends, and technology. In the past, Mormon missionaries used flannel graphs to illustrate their message. Today, they have professionally produced films on DVD. By the time you read this, they will probably have gone completely digital using some sort of computer tablet or projection tool. Are you relevant or speaking another language?

66

Something for everyone is something for no one

In the late 1990s, I had the unfortunate opportunity to own a Ford Taurus. It was one of the most popular sedans at the time, but I never understand why. In my opinion, the car didn't possess any exceptional qualities or features. However, the vehicle's "averageness" is the explanation to its success. Ford created a car that would appeal (to some extent) to the masses. When you make something unique, limit the number of people who will want it.

Unfortunately, whenever you create something that everyone will like, you also have to water it down to the point that everyone is OK with it but no one will LOVE it. In other words, to get the largest consensus you end up compromising, which reduces excitement, attraction, and interest. This approach also limits your creativity, depth, reach, impact, quality, uniqueness, and more. So, you have to ask whether you want a large group with low appreciation or a small group with high appreciation.

I would rather see you create something that attracts a smaller group who is crazy about you rather than appeals to the masses slightly.

67

Communication changes

One of my first jobs in marketing was designing faxes. Yes, there was a time when people sent faxes to businesses as a means of advertising. The introduction of marketing email quickly killed the fax, which I was very pleased about since faxes could only be designed in black and white (very boring). Our communication styles and methods evolve over time.

Technology, economics, culture, politics, and a thousand other things influence the way we distribute, receive and interpret information. Everything changed with the introduction of the printing press, radio, television, and internet. To maximize your communication, you need to take into account the present approaches, tools, and means in which people pass information. How are you responding to recent changes in communication, media, or technology? Are you even aware of such trends and advancements? What can you do to stay current?

Change is not as simple as following the crowd. Successful communication is NOT the result of merely following tradition OR doing what is popular.

Be cautious of any action that is solely motivated or supported by the statements as, "This is what everyone else is doing," or "This is what we've always done." Evaluate popular methods of communication and decide which are the best forms for you and your audience. Because something is working for others doesn't mean that it will work for you. Trends, by definition, will come and go. Build on the foundational principles of communication and remain flexible to present patterns when they are right for your situation.

Also, avoid the trap of maintenance (doing things just because you did them before). Tradition has a powerful influence on our actions because change can require more work and may cause friction from people's expectations and preferences. Transitions may not be easy, but successful communication continually looks at whether previous approaches continue to be effective. When you decide to make changes, be tactful because transitions can be uncomfortable. Evolve slowly and with a certain level of transparency.

68

Keep it simple

We used to have a television remote with a button labeled CALENDAR on it. All it did was superimpose a simple calendar across the screen, which had nothing to do with the television programming or planning. My best guess is that some engineer (or probably a committee) believed that the more features a television had the better it would be. Therefore, they tried to think of anything they could add to it (even if it had nothing to do with watching television).

During the life of that television, I don't recall one time that we needed the calendar mode. No one ever asked "Hey, what day is it?" I never had a chance to say, "You're in luck! I have a highly advanced television with a revolutionary calendar feature built right into it."

Even though we never needed the calendar, we saw it repeatedly. I would often accidentally hit the stupid calendar button since it was right next to another key that I used frequently (the keys were small; probably because they needed to make room for all the "great" features like calendar). Sometimes we make things more complex than they need to be just because we can. These unnecessary additions can cause frustration, delays, confusion, and worse.

Keep things simple. Make functionality and efficiency (speed) a priority. Like most television remotes, complexity can result in confusion. Is it necessary? Give them what they really need over everything you could provide.

69

Design matters

Even though buying digital books may save some trees and be the most convenient way to store and access an entire library of books, I still love the experience and feel of a good hardcover (or paperback) book. I especially like to see them in the bookcases of my home (even if I haven't read them all).

The biggest reason why I will probably always have "real" books is that I am a sucker for a good cover design. In other words, I judge books by their covers. Yes, I know that we have been told not to, but I can't help thinking some books are better just because of how they look. I do the same thing when buying all sorts of products: soap, bread, birdseed, paper, whatever (I am a sucker for good design).

Design is powerful, and people will make judgements about you based on the look and feel of your website, logo, color scheme, print advertising, and more. Design is often the first impression people will have of you. A poor design can distort, distract, and bury your message, mission, and identity. Your use (or lack of) imagery, fonts, color, and a hundred other design variables all have powerful influences on how people "feel" about and interpret your communication. If you are serious about how you communicate, then you need to place a very high value and focus on design.

Let me also say this. YOU ARE NOT AN ARTIST! I'm sure some of you are, but most people don't know the important principles behind creating an effective and accurate design. Make sure that if you are limited by time and talent that you empower the right people to design for you.

Using unqualified volunteers, clipart, or your sister's kid who seems to know more about computers than you do, can ultimately lead to a watered-down impression of who you are and what you do. So, how does your book cover look?

70

The last person without a cell phone

I don't like cell phones. Besides my paranoid fears about them causing cancer, I don't care for how the cell phone has changed things. I fully embraced the time when we kept them stored away in our cars (remember, you had to plug it into the cigarette lighter and leave the window cracked open for the magnetic roof antenna's cord to run into the car?). It was very inconvenient, so you only used them in case of an emergency. Today, people can't go anywhere without their phone or imagine not being able to contact someone no matter where they are or what they are doing.

I know this opinion sounds like a rant you couldn't care less about, but stick with me here because it does relate to business practices, eventually.

A few years ago, I noticed that while away from the office, I would check my phone every few minutes to read email. Almost every one of those emails didn't require an action until I was back in my office the next day. I was taking time away from more important things (such as my wife and kids) to give my attention to something that could wait. Cell phones often disrupt our attention from or communication with the present and redirect it somewhere else.

Have you ever answered your cell phone (or looked to see who was calling) while in a meeting, during a conversation, or in front of a customer? What does that say to those people? "I'm sorry, but this person is really more important than you and what we are doing here." It's as if no one has voicemail.

Now, consider the opposite. How would you feel if someone you were meeting, talking, or eating with said, "Just a minute, let turn my phone off because I want to give you my full attention."

Where is your attention? Maybe, you don't answer the phone in front of your customers, but is there anything else distracting you? Do they feel like they have your undivided attention? Do they feel like your conversation or work with them is the most important thing you could be doing at that moment? Perhaps, you need to "unplug" around them. In case you are curious, our family does own one cell phone, which we keep in the car.

71

Greatest burger in the world

A few months ago, I dined at a common chain restaurant whose menu stated "Greatest Burger in the World." Do they really have the "Greatest Burger?" It seemed a bit out of place since they serve all kinds of dishes (i.e, hamburgers are NOT their specialty). My wife asked me who I thought made the best hamburger...maybe she thinks I am some kind of hamburger connoisseur since that is what I tend to order when pizza isn't on the menu.

Well, you can get a fantastic bison burger at Ted's, but I also love Liam's Angus Burger. My dad makes a great homemade burger on the grill, but he is not open to the public. Chili's was my pick when I lived in Orlando and Texas. Once I had an amazing burger and potatoes for brunch at small cafe in Florida, but the one I had there last week wasn't that good. There is something nostalgic about The Varsity and even McDonalds (if you grew up on them like me). My mom swears nothing can compete with Steak 'n Shake. Plus, some say Fuddruckers is at the top of their list while others tell me the "Cheeseburger in Paradise" at Jimmy Buffets' Margaritaville is unbelievable. I even read an article in Time Magazine about the world's best burger being in EGYPT!

So who makes "The Greatest Burger in the World?"

This question is not easy to answer. Burger supremacy depends on the consumer, his/her preferences and exposure to what's available, who is cooking that day, and a hundred other variables. To be honest, my opinion may even be different tomorrow. However, I will let you know who is NOT the greatest: the guy who has to tell you he is. There is no need to tell people you are great (unless you really aren't and think you can convince them with just a caption).

Instead of telling people you are the greatest, make sure you ARE the greatest...and THEY will tell everyone else. Do people think you make the best hamburger (or whatever you do)? If not, what do you need to change so that others do?

72

Think like a Porsche

The Porsche 911 Turbo Cabriolet is very expensive to purchase ($140,700) and maintain. It's not built for luggage space, family vacations, off-roading, or good gas mileage. It's a very impractical vehicle to own.

However, the performance, design, and experience a Porsche offers overshadows its limitations. In other words, people buy a Porsche not for value but for the WOW. Or you could say that they purchase it because they value WOW.

What is it that you offer (or could offer) that people could consider to be WOW? And YES, value, practicality, and price can actually be considered WOW (that was Sam Walton's approach with Walton's Five and Dime, a precursor to Wal-Mart). The point is to make sure you are doing something that is WOW.

Are you thinking like a Porsche?

72

Now what?

I could supply you with a new observation or insight every day, but I think by now you should have a feel for what it takes to avoid average. My conclusion is rather simple: GO! You have so much potential and the opportunity is wide open to create remarkable things. Don't compromise or settle for anything less than exceptional in everything you do. Follow your passions, seek to rise above the average, and ***be extraordinary!***